VERBAL REASONING

GRADED TEST PAPERS 2

Susan J. Daughtrey M.Ed

Childs World Education

Revised 2011

ACKNOWLEDGEMENTS

I would like to thank my children Sara and James who enthusiastically contributed many ideas and performed numerous practical exercises. Also a special thanks to my students who (often unknowingly) provided the inspiration and feedback which has been so encouraging.

ISBN 978 1 898696 93 3

Published by Childs World Education, PO Box 1881, Gerrards Cross, Bucks SL9 9AN.

Printed in Great Britain by Halstan & Co Ltd, Plantation Road, Amersham, Bucks HP6 6HJ.

First published 1993.
First edition 1993.
Reprinted 1994, 1995, 1996 (twice), 1997, 1998, 1999, 2000, 2001, 2002, 2004, 2006, 2007, 2008, 2011, 2012, 2017.
Revised 2001, 2006, 2007, 2011.

For more information about these and other books and test packs by the same author and for details about Susan Daughtrey Education courses please visit:

www.SusanDaughtreyEducation.com

GRADED TEST PAPER 6

NAME . . . .

DATE . . . .

Instructions:

1. Allow 50 minutes for this Test.

2. Work quickly and accurately in PENCIL.

3. Always write NEATLY. If you need to change an answer cross out clearly so your examiner can see easily what you intend your answer to be. Do not use an eraser.

4. Always read the instructions of EACH question carefully so you know precisely what you are expected to do. Underline or write your answer in the brackets provided.

5. Use the edges of the pages for the Technique/working out.

6. Try to answer ALL the questions. Remember you can only get marks for the questions you answer!

7. Do not spend longer than 30 seconds on any question you cannot do. Move on. Keep up your speed. Don't get behind.

8. Circle the number of any question you miss out. When you finish your paper, return quickly to these. Do these first. Finally, return to the beginning of the paper. Check rigorously all your answers.

   Remember: CHECKING MEANS RETHINKING.

9. Your Examiner should tell you when you are half way through, 10 minutes, 5 minutes, 2 minutes and 1 minute to go.

10. Use all the 50 minutes. DO NOT stop working or checking until you are told to stop.

SCORE:

The three numbers in each group are related in the same way. Two groups have been completed for you. Find the rule that connects them and complete the third group of numbers in the same way by writing your answer in the brackets. Here is an example:

	2	(7)	14	7	(3)	21	4	(_5_)	20
1.	9	(10)	11	18	(14)	10	16	(___)	8
2.	40	(16)	8	20	(7)	6	30	(___)	6
3.	30	(15)	6	24	(13)	8	45	(___)	5
4.	3	(13)	4	4	(21)	5	8	(___)	3
5.	4	(14)	5	3	(19)	8	5	(___)	10
6.	18	(6)	3	30	(10)	5	40	(___)	7

David is 2 years older than Pat who is 4 years younger than Jo. Mary, who will be 17 next year, is twice the age of Pat. Now answer the following questions:

7. How old is David? . . . .   (_______)

8. How old is Jo? . . . .   (_______)

9. How much younger than Mary is David? . . . .   (_______)

10. How old will Pat be when Jo is as old as Mary is now? .   (_______)

11. How old will David be then? . . . .   (_______)

A, B, C, D and E are 5 cars. A, C and D have automatic gears, the others have manual gears. A and E are sports cars while the others are saloons. B and C seat 6 people, the others seat 4. Only B, D and E have sunroofs. Now circle the correct answers in the brackets:

12. Which car with automatic gears seats
    4 people and has a sunroof?   (A   B   C   D   E)

13. Which sports car seats 4 people and has
    manual gears?   (A   B   C   D   E)

14. Which 4 seater saloon car has a sunroof?   (A   B   C   D   E)

15. Which saloon with automatic gears
    seats 6 people?   (A   B   C   D   E)

16. How many cars with a sun roof have
    manual gears?   (__________________)

In each question below, underline the ONE word on the SECOND line that will go equally well with BOTH PAIRS of words in the brackets. Here is an example:

(flat   horizontal)   (standard   stage)
base   *level*   platform   phase   plain

17. (skin   pelt)   (conceal   obscure)
hide   mask   feathers   veil   fur

18. (attach   connect)   (snag   problem)
join   obstacle   clip   hitch   hook

19. (ribbon   strap)   (ensemble   orchestra)
group   company   band   belt   tie

20. (tatter   unstitch)   (fight   argument)
brawl   scrap   threadbare   tussle   fray

21. (elevate   lift)   (crane   winch)
hoist   heave   boost   pulley   raise

Here you must find the FOUR-letter word which is hidden BETWEEN the words in each of the following sentences. Write this word in the brackets. Here is an example:

Scientific paper*s and* books . . . . (_*sand*_)

22. Don't ask for any more money . . . .   (___________)

23. She came yesterday but I was out. . . . .   (___________)

24. What is meant by scuttling a ship?. . . . .   (___________)

25. Will you come at the weekend? . . . .   (___________)

26. Girls are made of all things nice . . . .   (___________)

27. Open the door immediately . . . .   (___________)

The table below shows the number of marks out of 150 which five girls scored in English tests for the years 1988 to 1992:

	Sophie	Rachel	Joanna	Gemma	Zoe
1988	123	68	74	90	63
1989	94	80	106	106	88
1990	132	59	63	97	79
1991	81	70	65	89	126
1992	128	57	108	69	81

Now answer the following questions by circling the correct answer in the brackets:

28.   In which year did Rachel score more than Joanna?
(1988,   89,   90,   91,   92)

29.   In which year did Sophie score less than Zoe?
(1988,   89,   90,   91,   92)

30.   Which girl scored her highest mark when 2
of the others scored their lowest?   (S   R   J   G   Z)

31.   Which two girls had their lowest mark in 1992
and their highest mark in 1989?   (S   R   J   G   Z)

32.   Which girl had her lowest mark coming
immediately after her highest?   (S   R   J   G   Z)

33.   Which girl had the smallest variation in
marks scored?   (S   R   J   G   Z)

34.   How many girls scored their highest marks
before their lowest?   (1   2   3   4   5)

35.   Which 2 girls scored their highest mark in the
same year?   (S   R   J   G   Z)

One letter from the word on the left-hand side must be taken and placed into or added to the word on the right-hand side so that TWO new and proper words are formed which are correctly spelt. All the other letters must remain in the same position. Here is an example:

C O U L D and B O N D become (_C O L D_) and (_B O U N D_)

36.   P A C T   and   P A T H   become   (__________) and (__________)

37.   S A N G   and   L A C E   become   (__________) and (__________)

38.   D I C E   and   D A N E   become   (__________) and (__________)

39.   C A R T   and   G E M   become   (__________) and (__________)

40. G A U N T   and   B A R E   become   (__________) and (__________)

41. H E R O N   and   D O Z E   become   (__________) and (__________)

42. N E I C E   and   P A C E   become   (__________) and (__________)

---

43.   **If S T E A M contains the fifth letter of the alphabet write X, unless C L O C K contains the eleventh letter of the alphabet in which case write Z.**   (__________)

---

44.   **My watch is 8 minutes fast and the bus which should have arrived at 4.49 p.m. is 6 minutes late. What time does my watch show when the bus arrives?**   (_________ p.m._)

All the following questions are concerned with numbers. Write your answer in the brackets. Here is an example:

15 is 3 more than half this number. . . (_24_)

45.   96 is 12 times larger than this number. . . . .   (______)

46.   If I add 6 to this number and subtract 9 the answer is 29. What is the number? . . . .   (______)

47.   Twice 12 is the same as three times a number. What is the number? . . . .   (______)

48.   If half of this number is three quarters of 24 what is twice the number? . . . .   (______)

49.   Three times this number plus 7 is 55. . . . .   (______)

There is a connection between the 2 words on the outside of the brackets and TWO of the words inside the brackets. Underline the two words. Here is an example:

NEEDLES PINS   (pine, *thread,* cramp, *thimble,* cut)

50. DOG HAMSTER ... (badger, black, doll, cat, pet)

51. CROCUS TULIP ... (garden, bulb, daffodil, snowdrop, spring)

52. ELBOW HIP...... (muscle, knee, cap, joint, wrist)

53. SIGHT SMELL .... (nose, eyes, touch, ear, taste)

54. IRON SILVER ..... (coal, metal, gold, aluminium, kettle)

55. TEACHER LAWYER (work, doctor, job, accountant, office)

56. TEA COFFEE ..... (water, sandwich, lunch, wine, snack)

57. SHOE COAT .... (hanger, hat, wardrobe, dress, cloakroom)

If A = 6, B = 5, C = 3, D = 2 and E = 1 find the value of the following :

58. $\dfrac{2 \times A}{C}$ Give your answer as a NUMBER . . . .   (______)

59. Which THREE letters added together give A as the answer?   (______)

60. Which TWO letters when multiplied together give A
as the answer? . . . .   (______)

61. Subtract E from C, multiply the answer by D and add E.
Give your answer as a LETTER . . . .   (______)

62. Divide A by D and add C. Give your answer as a LETTER.   (______)

One of the words in each of the following sentences has THREE consecutive letters missing. Without changing the order of these three letters they spell another proper word. Write this word in the brackets. Here is an example:

~~millions~~
There are mions of people in London. .(_*ill*_)

63. The kitten was as light as a fher . . . .   (________)

64. He dressed the wound with a bage . . . .   (________)

65. The sign read 'bars are not allowed in the fountain'. . . . .   (_________)

66. She rranged the books on the shelf . . . .   (_________)

67. He made a coueous attempt to rescue the drowning man .   (_________)

68. The buds will remain dort until the spring . . . .   (_________)

69. The rerch student made the final discovery . . . .   (_________)

70. He took it all in his ste . . . .   (_________)

71. The suit was made of a fine woven ch . . . .   (_________)

Below there are 5 groups of words labelled A, B, C, D and E. There is a connection between each member of each group, but there is no connection between the different groups.

A	B	C	D	E
hockey	Mersey	beech	Spain	shoal
football	Humber	elm	France	litter
netball	Thames	oak	Germany	flock

Below are 9 words. Identify the group to which each one belongs and write the letter of this group in the brackets next to the word.

72. larch   (____)   73. pack   (____)   74. Africa (____)

75. sycamore (____)   76. lacrosse (____)   77. pride   (____)

78. Severn   (____)   79. Tyne   (____)   80. Mexico (____)

A B C D E F G H I J K L M N O P Q R S T U V W X Y Z

The above alphabet is to help you with the following code questions. Write the answers in the brackets. Here is an example:

If G B S N means F A R M what does N J M L mean. . . (_MILK_)

81. If F L D Q means C O A T then O B D C means . .   (_________)

82. If C H R N means D E S K then S E A T is . . . . . .   (_________)

83. If E A S T is written V Z H G then W E S T is . . .   (_________)

84. If L E A F is written F F A E E L then W A L L is .   (_________)

85. If 16 K 14 G means P I N E then 4 Q 15 T means.   (_________)

86. If F O U R is written H M W P then N I N E is . .   (_________)

Underline the word which would come in the MIDDLE if the following were put in order of size, sequence or position. Here is an example:

(ninth   sixteenth   first   *sixth*   third)

87.   (day   week   second   minute   year)

88.   (country   town   village   hamlet   city)

89.   (one   thousand   million   ten   hundred)

90.   (99   91   19   33   577)

91.   (July   June   March   August   May)

92.   (06.30   00.08   1 a.m.   4.30 p.m.   noon)

Write in brackets the word needed to complete the third pair of words. This pair follows the same pattern as the first two pairs of words. Here is an example:

stone tone   /   slate late   /   cream (_ream_)

93.   ship hip   /   chop hop   /   them   (____________)

94.   jackpot top   /   magnet ten   /   spectator (____________)

95.   pride rid   /   stare tar   /   stint   (____________)

96.   dents ten   /   ladle lad   /   lease   (____________)

97.   swing wings   /   stray trays   /   scare   (____________)

98.   trail lit   /   brain nib   /   donor   (____________)

99.   truck cut   /   brush sub   /   trash   (____________)

100.   palm lamp   /   ripe pier   /   sent   (____________)

YOU HAVE COMPLETED THE TEST

GO BACK AND CHECK

REMEMBER : CHECKING MEANS RETHINKING

G R A D E D   T E S T   P A P E R   7

NAME . . . .

DATE . . . .

Instructions:

1. Allow 50 minutes for this Test.

2. Work quickly and accurately in PENCIL.

3. Always write NEATLY. If you need to change an answer cross out clearly so your examiner can see easily what you intend your answer to be. Do not use an eraser.

4. Always read the instructions of EACH question carefully so you know precisely what you are expected to do. Underline or write your answer in the brackets provided.

5. Use the edges of the pages for the Technique/working out.

6. Try to answer ALL the questions. Remember you can only get marks for the questions you answer!

7. Do not spend longer than 30 seconds on any question you cannot do. Move on. Keep up your speed. Don't get behind.

8. Circle the number of any question you miss out. When you finish your paper, return quickly to these. Do these first. Finally, return to the beginning of the paper. Check rigorously all your answers.

    Remember: CHECKING MEANS RETHINKING.

9. Your Examiner should tell you when you are half way through, 10 minutes, 5 minutes, 2 minutes and 1 minute to go.

10. Use all the 50 minutes. DO NOT stop working or checking until you are told to stop.

SCORE:

Each of the following pairs of brackets has ONE word which does not belong to the rest. Underline this 'odd one out'.

1.   (complete   partial   whole   entire   total)

2.   (destitute   affluent   rich   wealthy   prosperous)

3.   (opponent   foe   rival   adversary   ally)

4.   (deluge   flood   torrent   drought   surge)

5.   (abundance   scarcity   wealth   profusion   surplus)

6.   (beckon   summon   dismiss   invite   request)

7.   (gesture   motion   wave   signal   hand)

8.   (strange   normal   unusual   curious   weird)

In a secret code W S X O P Y N D B G P S X stands for C O N S I D E R A T I O N. Using the same code word work out how the following words should be written:

9.   C O R O N A T I O N . . . .   (________________)

10.   D I S T R I C T . . . .   (________________)

11.   T R E N D . . . .   (________________)

12.   D E C I S I O N . . . .   (________________)

Using the same code word work out what the following code words say:

13.   Y P O G D P W G . . . .   (________________)

14.   O W B X X N D . . . .   (________________)

15.   W S G G S X . . . .   (________________)

16.   G D B P X . . . .   (________________)

---

17.   **My watch is 8 minutes slow and the 6.47 p.m. train
      from Doncaster is 17 minutes late. What time
      does my watch say when the train arrives?**   (____________ p.m.__)

Find the FOUR-letter word which is hidden in each of the following sentences. Each four-letter word can be found by studying the letters at the end of one word and the beginning of the next word. Write this word in the brackets. Here is an example:

Scientific paper*s and* books . . . (_*sand*_)

18.   We miss it every time . . . .   (______________)

19.   The calf is hurt . . . .   (______________)

20.   The cab left the boy behind . . . .   (______________)

21.   He is writing on expensive paper . . . .   (______________)

22.   The pop group is on tour again . . . .   (______________)

23.   Come and see us soon . . . .   (______________)

In the questions below there are two pairs of letters that are related in some way. Write in the brackets the pair of letters that completes the second relationship in the same way. Here is an example:

A C   is to   B D   as   M O   is to   (_NP_)

24.   D V   is to   F T   as   C Y   is to   (________)

25.   I Z   is to   G V   as   H X   is to   (________)

26.   B N   is to   F J   as   E K   is to   (________)

27.   C E   is to   K J   as   G I   is to   (________)

28.   C D   is to   X W   as   K L   is to   (________)

29.   D H   is to   Y M   as   B K   is to   (________)

Each of the following has one word with its letters jumbled up. Using the 'clue', rearrange the letters and write the correct word in the brackets. Here is an example:

D W F A R R O   Opposite to reverse . . .(_FORWARD_)

30.   E G P N O S   Used to wash your face . .   (______________)

31.   N T E I R T E H   Is a number . . . .   (______________)

32.   T N G Y C E   A baby bird . . . .   (______________)

33.   W B G L A U N O   A type of dwelling. . . . . . .   (______________)

34.   A K O S D E   Thoroughly wet through .   (______________)

35.   U N O R Y P A G L D   A safe place to play. . . . . .   (______________)

**In the following questions write in the brackets the ONE letter
which will finish the first word and begin the second. The same
letter is used for both pairs of words. Here is an example:**

B O O (*T*) A K E : L A S (*T*) R A C K

36.   F L O (___) O N   :   C R E (___) E T

37.   L O O (___) A I N   :   S N A (___) E T

38.   B A (___) O N E   :   P L A (___) U L L

39.   R A (___) E A R   :   S A (___) E L

40.   S T A (___) E A R   :   B R A (___) O U R

41.   L A N (___) A R N   :   A R (___) A S T

**Underline one word in each pair of brackets in order to make the
most sensible sentence:**

42.   (While, What, Where) is the (book, boy, rabbit) who lost his
       (building, tortoise, sky) ?

43.   The (bicycle, aeroplane, cat) made a smooth (nest, pillow, landing)
       on the (tree, runway, bedroom).

44.   The (robot, school boy, housewife) put his (cap, horse, desk) on his
       (pocket, stable, head).

45.   The (choir, wind, nightingale) sang a (music, song, composer) at the
       (orchestra, rhapsody, concert).

**There is a connection between the 3 words on the outside of the
brackets and TWO of the words inside the brackets. Underline the
two words. Here is an example:**

QUEEN LADY MOTHER (king lord *aunt* prince *princess*)

46.   GIRAFFE   MONKEY   ELEPHANT (pig   hen   cheetah   dog   lion)

47.   DEN   DREY   SET . . . . (tent   nest   warren   pack   house)

48.   CAP   BOWLER   STETSON . (beret   gun   sombrero   cricket   head)

49.   SYCAMORE   ASH   LARCH . . . . . . (tree   oak   pine   key   forest)

50. HOCKEY LACROSSE CRICKET . (snooker ludo game pitch golf)

51. ELBOW ANKLE KNEE . . . . (limb joint body shoulder hip)

52. MARS SARTURN PLUTO . . . (earth sun star planet Venus)

Write in the brackets the word needed to complete the third pair of words. This pair follows the same pattern as the first two pairs of words. Here is an example:

heir her / baby bay / pain (_pan_)

53.	laden lead	/	baker beak	/	pater	(____________)
54.	suit situ	/	team tame	/	meal	(____________)
55.	beat feat	/	save wave	/	hook	(____________)
56.	stop hops	/	slit hits	/	seat	(____________)
57.	neat mate	/	team same	/	heat	(____________)
58.	star rats	/	step pets	/	part	(____________)
59.	hair hire	/	fair fire	/	suit	(____________)
60.	tariff fair	/	motors root	/	sepals	(____________)

The number codes for three of the following four words are given below. These codes are not written in the same order as the words and one of the codes is missing.

TRAP   PEAR   TEAR   RATE
5432   6245   3546

Work out the correct code for each word and answer the following questions by writing your answer in the brackets.

61. What is the missing code? . . . . (____________)

62. What word has the number code 5432? . . . . (____________)

63. What is the code for the word TREAT? . . . . (____________)

64. What is the code for the word PART? . . . . (____________)

65. What word has the number code 526243? . . . . . . (____________)

The three numbers in each group are related in the same way. Two groups have been completed for you. Find the rule that connects them and complete the third group of numbers in the same way by writing your answer in the brackets. Here is an example:

	2	(7)	14	7	(3)	21	4	(_5_)	20
66.	4	(8)	3	6	(12)	5	9	(___)	4
67.	3	(14)	4	6	(22)	5	9	(___)	4
68.	11	(18)	3	12	(17)	5	15	(___)	9
69.	15	(14)	8	16	(20)	6	19	(___)	4
70.	6	(10)	2	7	(10)	4	12	(___)	2
71.	24	(11)	3	30	(9)	5	27	(___)	3

The following are a type of crossword. Complete each puzzle by fitting the five words on the right-hand side of the grid horizontally and vertically into the correct positions. One word has been included already. Here is an example:

SAM
MEN
TEN   becomes
APE
SAT

S	A	M
A	P	E
T	E	N

72.

YON
SAT
AGO
SAY
AGE

73.

MAP
POT
AGO
AGE
NET

74.

ADO
ODE
ONE
GOD
AGO

75.

AND
NOW
TOO
ATE
EWE

76. If two days after tomorrow is Sunday, what is the second letter of the day which comes four days before today?

(__________)

77. **Which letter appears twice in T R A N S P A R E N T, twice in I N V I T A T I O N but only once in I N T R O S P E C T I V E?**   (__________)

In each of the following number series there is a different connection between the numbers. Find each connection and continue the series placing your answer in the brackets. Here is an example:

	1.5	**3**	**6**	**12**	**(_24_)**	**(_48_)**
78.	4	(___)	16	25	(___)	49
79.	4	4	8	24	(___)	480
80.	(___)	49	38	27	(___)	5
81.	96	(___)	24	12	(___)	3	1.5
82.	58	47	56	49	54	(___)	(___)
83.	31	(___)	36	40	45	51	(___)
84.	325	436	547	(___)	(___)

There are 5 books A, B, C, D and E on a shelf. E is one book from the right-hand end and has A immediately on its left. Two books to the right of A is C which is 4 books to the right of B.
Now answer the following questions:

85. Which book is in the middle? . . . .   (__________)

86. Which book is farthest left? . . . .   (__________)

87. Which books are on either side of A? . . . .   (__________)

Underline the word that would come in the MIDDLE if the following were put in order of size, sequence or position. Here is an example:

(thimble   jug   mug   <u>*cup*</u>   egg cup)

88. (64   46   644   446   614)

89. (00.45   16.25   11.05 p.m.   9.30 a.m.   06.15)

90. (melon   tomato   cherry   orange   grapefruit)

91. (pentagon   triangle   octogon   heptagon   rectangle)

92. (corporal   major   private   sergeant   colonel)

93. (cottage   mansion   palace   house   flat)

Below are set out the marks five boys scored in school tests. The maximum score for each test is written in brackets under each subject heading.

	Eng (20)	Maths (20)	Science (15)	Hist (20)	Geog (15)	Art (15)
David	16	20	14	18	12	10
Matthew	13	16	12	16	12	9
James	18	19	15	17	13	14
Tom	18	15	12	20	14	13
Mandeep	17	16	10	19	9	12

94. How many children scored full marks for a test? . . . . . (____________)

95. How many children were better in Maths than English ? . . . . (____________)

96. How many children scored fewer than 35 marks for English and Maths? . . . . (____________)

97. Which children scored higher in Maths than English or History ? . . . . (____________)

98. Which child had the smallest variation in marks in English, Maths and History? . . . . . . (____________)

99. Which child is better at Geography than Art or Science? . . . . (____________)

100. How many children did better in Science than Art? . . . . (____________)

YOU HAVE COMPLETED THE TEST

GO BACK AND CHECK

REMEMBER : CHECKING MEANS RETHINKING

ANSWERS

TEST PAPER 8:

1.	C	
2.	L	
3.	T	
4.	C	
5.	I	T15/2
6.	RMYOG	
7.	OGYPR	
8.	SYLGR	
9.	MGYOR	
10.	MASTS	
11.	STEAM	
12.	PATTER	T34/4
13.	all	
14.	ink or kin	
15.	ate	
16.	old	
17.	rim	
18.	den	
19.	lay	T20/2
20.	11.56 a.m.	T30/3
21.	beach	
22.	catkin	
23.	838	
24.	72	
25.	table	
26.	purse	
27.	tent	
28.	roars	
29.	outside	T12/1
30.	antler	
31.	decent	
32.	later	
33.	message	
34.	spread	
35.	patter	
36.	resemble	T14/2
37.	BEAD LEARN	
38.	SEAM TONE	
39.	LAND STABLE	
40.	FRIED DONOR	
41.	REAM MEDAL	
42.	CAMP SOLAR	T3/1
43.	person horse	
44.	trunk stem	
45.	clock wheel	
46.	driver pilot	
47.	happiness sorrow	
48.	hunger thirst	
49.	8 6	T2/1
50.	9	
51.	8	
52.	6	
53.	8	
54.	1	
55.	6	Equations
56.	12	
57.	10	
58.	9	
59.	Betty	T30/3
60.	19	
61.	43	
62.	24	
63.	36	
64.	5	T30/3
65.	O	T15/2
66.	howl	
67.	sail	
68.	cold	
69.	lout	
70.	hide	
71.	ream	
72.	epic	
73.	omen	
74.	item	T5/1
75.	28	
76.	8 2	
77.	70 50	
78.	269	
79.	62 73	
80.	24 15	
81.	36 81	
82.	47 95	T26/3
83.	numerous many	
84.	noisy rowdy	
85.	raise elevate	
86.	top summit	
87.	expand enlarge	
88.	expensive dear	
89.	receive accept	T7/1
90.	notelet	
91.	bandage	
92.	towing	
93.	rampage	
94.	notable	T4/1
95.	S	
96.	T	
97.	E	
98.	R	
99.	R	
100.	F	T21/2

TEST PAPER 9:

1.	encounter meet	
2.	lazy indolent	
3.	edible eatable	
4.	dry parched	
5.	succulent juicy	
6.	artificial false	T7/1
7.	Y F	
8.	N	
9.	H	
10.	QT	
11.	AX	
12.	N J	
13.	G T	T16/2
14.	PEST	
15.	NEAR	
16.	DUST	
17.	MOOD	
18.	LEAN	
19.	RUST	T22/2
20.	earwig	
21.	rotten	
22.	method	
23.	orbit	
24.	restless	
25.	noon	
26.	booklet	T4/1
27.	D	
28.	A B C D E	T15/2
29.	5 2 1 3 4	
30.	2 4 5 3 1	
31.	3 4 2 1 5	
32.	5 2 3 1 4	
33.	4 5 3 2 1	T17/2
34.	H	T15/2
35.	30	
36.	12	
37.	16	
38.	6	
39.	32	
40.	4	T28/3
41.	d	T31/4
42.	T	
43.	E	
44.	Y	
45.	T	
46.	E	
47.	H	
48.	T	
49.	L	T21/2
50.	TENT	
51.	TABLE	
52.	RING	
53.	KLHG	
54.	LADY	
55.	CAST	T32/4
56.	come lame	
57.	seventy hundred	
58.	wrote went	
59.	pale sale	
60.	aeroplane car	
61.	solid liquid	T2/1
62.	ill	
63.	ice	
64.	age	
65.	lid	
66.	too	
67.	pen	
68.	ear	
69.	bin	T20/2
70.	EAR BRING	
71.	TEAK SOUGHT	
72.	BEAD CART	
73.	CANE BOUT	
74.	SALE CLAY	
75.	SPED MOIST	T3/1
76.	12	
77.	DAVID	
78.	4 years	
79.	15	
80.	1	T30/3
81.	357358	
82.	85737	
83.	753358	
84.	TERROR	
85.	SORTER	
86.	ROOSTER	T33/4
87.	flee	
88.	red	
89.	range	
90.	mat	
91.	pay	
92.	pit	T8/1
93.	teacher	
94.	spread	
95.	street	
96.	portion	
97.	patch	T14/2
98.	PIP ARE YEN	
99.	ASK SEE HAG	
100.	LID ACE PEN	T9/1

Mary = 16   David = 8
Pat = 6   16
Jo = 10   4
               12

ANSWERS

TEST PAPER 6:

#	Answer	Ref
1.	12	
2.	12	
3.	19	
4.	25	
5.	25	
6.	13	T28/3
7.	10	
8.	12	
9.	6 years	
10.	12	
11.	14	T30/3
12.	D	
13.	E	
14.	D	
15.	C	
16.	2	T23/2
17.	hide	
18.	hitch	
19.	band	
20.	fray	
21.	hoist	T7/1
22.	task	
23.	eyes	
24.	gash	
25.	meat	
26.	fall	
27.	pent	T5/1
28.	91	
29.	91	
30.	J	
31.	R G	
32.	S	
33.	R	
34.	3	
35.	R G	T29/3
36.	PAT PATCH	
37.	SAG LANCE	
38.	DIE DANCE	
39.	CAT GERM	
40.	AUNT BARGE	
41.	HERO DOZEN	
42.	NICE PEACE	T3/1
43.	Z	T15/2
44.	5.03 p.m.	T30/3
45.	8	
46.	32	
47.	8	
48.	72	
49.	16	T24/3
50.	badger cat	
51.	daffodil snowdrop	
52.	knee wrist	
53.	touch taste	
54.	gold aluminium	
55.	doctor accountant	
56.	water wine	
57.	hat dress	T10/1
58.	4	
59.	C + D + E	
60.	C x D	
61.	B	
62.	A	T35/4
63.	eat	
64.	and	
65.	the	
66.	ear	
67.	rag	
68.	man	
69.	sea	
70.	rid	
71.	lot	T20/2
72.	C	
73.	E	
74.	D	
75.	C	
76.	A	
77.	E	
78.	B	
79.	B	
80.	D	T11/1
81.	LEAF	
82.	RHZW	
83.	DVHG	
84.	LLLAAW	
85.	DOOR	
86.	PGPC	T32/4
87.	day	
88.	town	
89.	hundred	
90.	91	
91.	June	
92.	06.30	T13/1
93.	hem	
94.	rot	
95.	tin	
96.	sea	
97.	cares	
98.	rod	
99.	sat	
100.	nets	T8/1

TEST PAPER 7:

#	Answer	Ref
1.	partial	
2.	destitute	
3.	ally	
4.	drought	
5.	scarcity	
6.	dismiss	
7.	hand	
8.	normal	T12/1
9.	WSDSXBGPSX	
10.	YPOGDPWG	
11.	GDNXY	
12.	YNWPOPSX	
13.	DISTRICT	
14.	SCANNER	
15.	COTTON	
16.	TRAIN	T34/4
17.	6.56 p.m.	T30/3
18.	site	
19.	fish	
20.	able	
21.	gone	
22.	onto	
23.	mean	T5/1
24.	EW	
25.	FT	
26.	IG	
27.	ON	
28.	PO	
29.	WP	T16/2
30.	SPONGE	
31.	THIRTEEN	
32.	CYGNET	
33.	BUNGALOW	
34.	SOAKED	
35.	PLAYGROUND	T19/2
36.	W	
37.	P	
38.	N	
39.	G	
40.	Y	
41.	E	T21/2
42.	Where boy tortoise	
43.	aeroplane landing runway	
44.	school boy cap head	
45.	choir song concert	T18/2
46.	cheetah lion	
47.	nest warren	
48.	beret sombrero	
49.	oak pine	
50.	snooker golf	
51.	shoulder hip	
52.	earth venus	T10/1
53.	peat	
54.	male	
55.	look	
56.	hats	
57.	gate	
58.	trap	
59.	site	
60.	leap	T8/1
61.	3245	
62.	RATE	
63.	35243	
64.	6453	
65.	REPEAT	T33/4
66.	14	
67.	26	
68.	16	
69.	30	
70.	22	
71.	12	T28/3
72.	SAY AGO TEN	
73.	MAP AGO NET	
74.	ADO GOD ONE	
75.	AND TOO EWE	T9/1
76.	u	
77.	N	T15/2
78.	9 36	
79.	96	
80.	60 16	
81.	48 6	
82.	51 52	
83.	33 58	
84.	658 769	T26/3
85.	A	
86.	B	
87.	D and E	T30/3
88.	446	
89.	9.30 a.m.	
90.	orange	
91.	pentagon	
92.	sergeant	
93.	house	T13/1
94.	3	
95.	3	
96.	3	
97.	David James	
98.	James	
99.	Tom	
100.	3	T29/3

c = automatic gear, b   A = automatic gear, sport car
people.   B = heat . . 6, sun . .

GRADED TEST PAPER 8

NAME . . . .

DATE . . . .

Instructions:

1. Allow 50 minutes for this Test.

2. Work quickly and accurately in PENCIL.

3. Always write NEATLY. If you need to change an answer cross out clearly so your examiner can see easily what you intend your answer to be. Do not use an eraser.

4. Always read the instructions of EACH question carefully so you know precisely what you are expected to do. Underline or write your answer in the brackets provided.

5. Use the edges of the pages for the Technique/working out.

6. Try to answer ALL the questions. Remember you can only get marks for the questions you answer!

7. Do not spend longer than 30 seconds on any question you cannot do. Move on. Keep up your speed. Don't get behind.

8. Circle the number of any question you miss out. When you finish your paper, return quickly to these. Do these first. Finally, return to the beginning of the paper. Check rigorously all your answers.

   Remember: CHECKING MEANS RETHINKING.

9. Your Examiner should tell you when you are half way through, 10 minutes, 5 minutes, 2 minutes and 1 minute to go.

10. Use all the 50 minutes. DO NOT stop working or checking until you are told to stop.

SCORE:

1. Which letter occurs once in CISTERN twice in CONCRETE
    and twice in INSIGNIFICANCE?   (________)

2. Which letter occurs three times in PARALLELOGRAM,
    twice in QUADRILATERAL and once in TRIANGLE?   (________)

3. Which letter occurs twice in NECESSITATE, twice in
    LITERATE but not at all in LIKELY or in DROLE?   (________)

4. Which letter occurs twice in SUCCESSIVE, twice in
    CIRCUIT but only once in CENTRE?   (________)

5. Which letter occurs twice as often in ABBREVIATION and
    MOUNTAINEERING as it does in LOCATION?   (________)

**In a secret code R X M G O P Y O L G S stands for
S U P E R M A R K E T. Using the same code, work out how the
following words should be written:**

6.   S P A R E . . . .   (__________________)

7.   R E A M S . . . .   (__________________)

8.   T A K E S . . . .   (__________________)

9.   P E A R S . . . .   (__________________)

**Now, using this same code work out what the following code words
stand for:**

10.   P Y R S R . . . .   (__________________)

11.   R S G Y P . . . .   (__________________)

12.   M Y S S G O . . . .   (__________________)

**One of the words in each of the following sentences has THREE
consecutive letters missing. Without changing the order of these
three letters they spell another proper word. Write this word in the
brackets. Here is an example:**

~~computer~~

The keyboard of my comer is broken . . . . (__ *put*__)

13. The leaves are fing off the trees. . . . .   (________)

14. The kitten is dring its milk . . . .   (________)

15. Can I have a glass of wr please ? . . . .   (________)

16. The sier is marching on parade . . . . (________)

17. The lines mark the peeter of the pitch . . . . (________)

18. The garer is cutting the lawn. . . . . (________)

19. The children are ping on the swings . . . . (________)

---

20. **My watch is eleven minutes fast and the train which should have arrived at 11.38 a.m. is 7 minutes late. What time does my watch say when the train arrives?** (________)

Each of the following pairs of brackets has ONE word which does not belong to the rest. Underline this 'odd one out'.

21. (oak   ash   beach   birch   elm)

22. (daffodil   primrose   violet   tulip   catkin)

23. (383   363   333   838   343)

24. (49   36   72   25   64)

25. (chair   stool   bench   sofa   table)

26. (tumbler   urn   vase   glass   purse)

27. (warren   tent   nest   set   den   drey)

28. (leaps   bounds   roars   runs   swings)

29. (outside   rim   border   edge   perimeter)

Underline the ONE word inside the brackets which CANNOT be made using the letters of the word outside the brackets.

30. PLEASANTLY   (steal   leaps   sepal   antler   peasant)

31. RESIDENCE   (nicer   desire   creed   denser   decent)

32. INSTALMENT   (stint   metal   later   taint   stain)

33. STRATAGEM   (great   master   treats   message   stream)

34. PROMISED   (prised   domes   spread   drop   prose)

35. PERMANENT   (manner   enter   parent   patter   meant)

36. MISERABLE   (blame   sable   resemble   reams   slime)

One letter from the word on the left-hand side must be taken and placed into or added to the word on the right-hand side so that TWO new and sensible words are formed which are correctly spelt. All the other letters must remain in the same position. Here is an example:

S C A R E and B O A T become (_CARE_) and (_BOAST_)

37. B R E A D and L E A N become (__________) and (__________)

38. S T E A M and O N E become (__________) and (__________)

39. B L A N D and S T A L E become (__________) and (__________)

40. F R I E N D and D O O R become (__________) and (__________)

41. D R E A M and M E A L become (__________) and (__________)

42. C L A M P and S O A R become (__________) and (__________)

In each of the following there is the SAME connection between the word outside the brackets and ONE word inside each pair of brackets. Underline these words, one word from each pair of brackets. Here is an example:

**Fruit is to (tree, *banana*, bowl) as
vegetable is to (*potato*, pie, meat)**

43. Foot is to (run, shoe, person) as hoof is to (cat, rider, horse)

44. Tree is to (leaf, root, trunk) as flower is to (colour, stem, flower)

45. Hand is to (fist, glove, clock) as spoke is to (speak, wheel, verse)

46. Bus is to (passenger, driver, stop) as aeroplane is to
(runway, flight, pilot)

47. Smile is to (face, happiness, teeth) as frown is to
(whisper, laughter, sorrow)

48. Food is to (eat, supper, hunger) as water is to (cold, thirst, run)

49. 4 is to (2, 8, 16) as 2 is to (6, 10, 20)

In these questions you must find the number that completes the sum correctly. Write your answers in the brackets. Here is an example:

6 + 6 = 9 + (_3_)

50. 4 x 6 + 3 = 9 x 4 – (______)

51. 108 ÷ 3 + 4 = 8 x 6 – (______)

52.　57　−　6　+　3　=　12　x　5　−　(＿＿＿)

53.　9　x　8　+　8　=　12　x　6　+　(＿＿＿)

54.　110　÷　10　−　6　=　24　÷　6　+　(＿＿＿)

55.　12　+　9　−　3　=　30　−　6　−　(＿＿＿)

In four years time Betty will be twice as old as Alice was last year. Sally, who will be 8 next year, is 2 years younger than Alice. Now answer the following questions:

56.　How old is Betty? . . . . (＿＿＿＿＿)

57.　How old will Sally be in 3 years time? . . . . (＿＿＿＿＿)

58.　How old is Alice now? . . . . (＿＿＿＿＿)

59.　Who is the oldest? . . . . (＿＿＿＿＿)

Seven years ago I was 12 years old and my father was then 3 times as old as I was. Now answer the following questions:

60.　How old am I now? . . . . (＿＿＿＿＿)

61.　How old is my father now? . . . . (＿＿＿＿＿)

62.　How old was my father when I was born? . . . . (＿＿＿＿＿)

63.　How old will I be when my father is 60? . . . . (＿＿＿＿＿)

64.　In how many years time will my father's age
　　 be twice mine? . . . . (＿＿＿＿＿)

65.　**If the day after tomorrow is Saturday what is
　　 the second letter of 2 days before yesterday?**　　(＿＿＿＿＿)

In the following sentences there is a FOUR-letter word hidden between words which are next to each other. Find the word and write it in the brackets. Here is an example:

Scientific paper*s and* books . . . . (＿*sand*＿)

66.　Do you know how late he will be? . . . . (＿＿＿＿＿＿)

67. His ailing body started to fail . . . . (__________)

68. He lived in a rustic old cottage . . . . (__________)

69. Don't fall out of the window . . . . (__________)

70. He didn't have much idea of how it worked . . . . (__________)

71. Both sisters were ambitious . . . . (__________)

72. Please hang the picture on the wall . . . . (__________)

73. He has arrived safely home now . . . . (__________)

74. The dress was made of white material . . . . (__________)

There is a different rule connecting each of the numbers in the following rows. Find the next number in each of the series and write it in the brackets.

75.   16   24   20   (___)   24   32

76.   512   128   32   (___)   (___)   0.5

77.   80   90   60   (___)   40   (___)

78.   625   536   447   358   (___)

79.   18   29   40   51   (___)   (___)

80.   80   63   48   35   (___)   (___)

81.   25   (___)   49   64   (___)

82.   2   5   11   23   (___)   (___)

There are two groups of words in each question below. Choose TWO words, one from each group which are CLOSEST in meaning to each other. Here is an example:

big / _wealthy_ / man : _rich_ / bank / beautiful

83.   often / numerous / grate   :   big / many / seldom

84.   noisy / party / sound   :   quiet / calm / rowdy

85.   down / raise / lower   :   elevate / bottom / under

86.   up / top / mountain   :   down / huge / summit

87.   conspire / expand / stay   :   go / enlarge / expire

88.	expensive / money / bill	:	cheap / change / dear
89.	receive / need / require	:	take / give / accept

A word on the left-hand side will join with a word on the right-hand side to form a completely new and proper word. The word on the left-hand side always begins this new word. Underline the two words, one from each group. Here is an example:

sit / will / *man*   :   now / *age* / ton

90.	aim / over / note	:	ring / let / tear
91.	band / or / get	:	age / gill / now
92.	now / sum / to	:	work / let / wing
93.	be / still / ram	:	less / page / sack
94.	port / cord / no	:	table / tail / head

In the following questions write in the brackets the ONE letter which will finish the first word and begin the second. The same letter is used for both pairs of words. Here is an example:

S E L (*F*) A M E   :   S H E L (*F*) E W

95.	M O S (___) I R E N	:	L O S (___) I C K
96.	C A S (___) U S K	:	L I S (___) R I P
97.	S O L (___) A G E R	:	M O L (___) A V E S
98.	B O A (___) U D E	:	S T A (___) O A D
99.	H E A (___) E N T	:	H E (___) E A R
100.	L E A (___) A M E	:	S E L (___) O G

YOU HAVE COMPLETED THE TEST

GO BACK AND CHECK

REMEMBER : CHECKING MEANS RETHINKING

GRADED TEST PAPER 9

NAME . . . .

DATE . . . .

Instructions:

1. Allow 50 minutes for this Test.

2. Work quickly and accurately in PENCIL.

3. Always write NEATLY. If you need to change an answer cross out clearly so your examiner can see easily what you intend your answer to be. Do not use an eraser.

4. Always read the instructions of EACH question carefully so you know precisely what you are expected to do. Underline or write your answer in the brackets provided.

5. Use the edges of the pages for the Technique/working out.

6. Try to answer ALL the questions. Remember you can only get marks for the questions you answer!

7. Do not spend longer than 30 seconds on any question you cannot do. Move on. Keep up your speed. Don't get behind.

8. Circle the number of any question you miss out. When you finish your paper, return quickly to these. Do these first. Finally, return to the beginning of the paper. Check rigorously all your answers.

   Remember: CHECKING MEANS RETHINKING.

9. Your Examiner should tell you when you are half way through, 10 minutes, 5 minutes, 2 minutes and 1 minute to go.

10. Use all the 50 minutes. DO NOT stop working or checking until you are told to stop.

SCORE:

Underline TWO words, one from each set of words, which have the SAME or nearly the same meaning. Here is an example:

expose exchange <u>*expand*</u> : engage <u>*enlarge*</u> endorse

1.	reveal encounter convince :	conspire contract meet
2.	lifeless lacking lazy :	idol indolent inspire
3.	legible audible edible :	drinkable eatable capable
4.	dry childlike ancient :	moist parched youth
5.	conceal succulent employ :	reveal juicy languish
6.	artificial edifice cheap :	expensive false bird

A B C D E F G H I J K L M N O P Q R S T U V W X Y Z

Using the above alphabet to help you, continue the letter series in each of the examples below, and fill in the empty brackets. Here is an example:

H   I   G   J   F   (_K_)   (_E_)

7.	G	J	N	S	(_____)	(_____)
8.	K	L	J	M	I	(_____)
9.	W	V	T	Q	M	(_____)
10.	A D	E H	I L	M P	(_____)	
11.	U D	P I	K N	F S	(_____)	
12.	M	(_____)	L	O	K	P	(_____)
13.	A	Z	C	X	E	V	(_____) (_____)

In the following there are two sets of words. The word in the brackets on the left-hand side has been formed using some of the letters of the words on either side of its brackets. You must write the missing word in the brackets on the right-hand side which has been formed from its pair of words in the same way. Here is an example:

COST (T O O K) POKE : HEIR (R E A R) PART

14.	CAST (S T U N) UPON :	TAPE (________) SOOT
15.	CARE (R E S T) STUN :	CANE (________) ARID

16. SICK (K I N G) HANG   :   CURD (________) REST

17. FORK (R O O F) ROPE   :   DOME (________) BAND

18. REST (S T E P) TRIP   :   HALT (________) EVEN

19. SEAT (S E N D) SAND   :   RULE (________) VEST

A word on the left-hand side will join together with a word on the right-hand side to form a completely new and proper word. The word on the left-hand side always begins this new word. Underline the two words, one from each group. Here is an example:

sit / will / *man* : now / *age* / ton

20.   sit / hand / ear   :   man / wig / ham

21.   rot / so / cat   :   ten / ice / led

22.   fur / met / more   :   log / in / hod

23.   mist / or / can   :   err / bit / rim

24.   get / on / rest   :   full / less / her

25.   no / if / now   :   yon / on / say

26.   fall / book / had   :   off / let / into

---

27. **Which letter in the word CRADLE has the same place in the alphabet as it does in the word?**   (________)

---

28. **Write in alphabetical order the five letters in the word BLANCHED which are consecutive in the alphabet.** (________)

Put the following in alphabetical order by writing your answers 1, 2, 3, 4 or 5 in the brackets.

29. plight ( )   plank ( )   planet ( )   play ( )   pliers ( )

30. frank ( )   fright ( )   fry ( )   frigate ( )   frame ( )

31. oasis ( )   oat ( )   oars ( )   oak ( )   ogre ( )

32. minute ( )   midget ( )   mind ( )   middle ( )   mint ( )

33. strap ( )   strut ( )   strand ( )   stop ( )   stamp ( )

34.　**If two days after tomorrow is Thursday what is the second letter of the day which is three days before yesterday?**　　(________)

The three numbers in each group are related in the same way. Two groups have been completed for you. Find the rule that connects them and complete the third group of numbers in the same way by writing your answer in the brackets. Here is an example:

	2	(7)	14	7	(3)	21	4	(_5_)	20
35.	6	(30)	4	5	(41)	7	3	(___)	8
36.	30	(10)	6	48	(12)	8	54	(___)	9
37.	4	(12)	4	9	(21)	3	6	(___)	4
38.	10	(4)	2	30	(9)	12	18	(___)	6
39.	20	(30)	3	18	(27)	3	16	(___)	4
40.	8	(3)	12	3	(10)	15	11	(___)	22

41.　**If Thomas, the tom cat, is older than Felix but younger than William then underline the one statement below which MUST be true:**

　　a.　Thomas is the youngest.
　　b.　Felix is the oldest.
　　c.　Thomas is the nicest.
　　d.　William is the oldest.

In the following questions write in the brackets the ONE letter which will finish the first word and begin the second word of each pair. The same letter is used for both pairs of words. Here is an example:

BOO (_T_) AKE : LAS (_T_) RACK

42.	C A R (___) U R N	:	S L A N (___) H E F T
43.	T A L (___) A G E R	:	C U R (___) A R
44.	S T A (___) O L K	:	C L A (___) O U R
45.	B E S (___) I P	:	B E L (___) A M E
46.	M A R (___) A R	:	F O R (___) L O P E
47.	B O T (___) O L D	:	C A S (___) O L E

48.   H A L (___) E A K   :   S E A (___) R A M

49.   P A I (___) A R D   :   T O I (___) O U D

A B C D E F G H I J K L M N O P Q R S T U V W X Y Z

The above alphabet will help you to find the answers to the following code questions. Write your answers in the brackets. Here is an example:

If K V N Q means J U M P then T U P Q means. . .(_STOP_)

50.   If D Z N O means C A M P then U D O S means . .   (______________)

51.   If 6 D 1 T 20 means F E A S T then 20 Z 2 M 5 means (______________)

52.   If Y V O O means B E L L then I R M T means . . .   (______________)

53.   If S T A M P is written H G Z N K then P O S T
      is written . . . .   (______________)

54.   If M A A B N C means M A N then
      L A A B D C Y means . . . .   (______________)

55.   If E 21 T 20 stands for D U S T what is D 1 T 20. . .   (______________)

In each of the following, there is the SAME connection between the word outside each set of brackets and one word inside each set of brackets. You must find this same connection and underline the two words, one from each set of brackets. Here is an example:

Car is to (_road_, wheel, garage) as barge is to (coal, lock, _canal_)

56.   Comb is to (hair, come, teeth) as lamb is to (sheep, wool, lame)

57.   Seven is to (seventeen, seventy, six) as ten is to
                                    (hundred, thousand, one)

58.   Write is to (pen, letter, wrote) as go is to (went, leave, come)

59.   Pail is to (bucket, pale, water) as Sail is to (sea, yacht, sale)

60.   Pilot is to (aeroplane, captain, airport) as driver is to
                                    (car, road, licence)

61.   Ice is to (cold, winter, solid) as water is to (wet, liquid, river)

One of the words in each of the following sentences has THREE consecutive letters missing. Without changing the order of these three letters they spell another proper word. Write this word in the brackets. Here is an example:

~~crowded~~
The fans cded around the pop-star . . . (_row_)

62. There are mions of people in London . . . . (________)

63. The television lnse has expired . . . . (________)

64. Are you able to man all by yourself? . . . . (________)

65. It is so cold the milk has frozen so. . . . . (________)

66. She misk her for someone else . . . . (________)

67. The oranges were left in the sun to ri . . . . (________)

68. She managed to get nly all the sums right. . . . . (________)

69. The china caet was full of pretty plates . . . . (________)

One letter from the word on the left-hand side must be taken and placed into or added to the word on the right-hand side so that TWO new and sensible words are formed which are correctly spelt. All the other letters must remain in the same position. Here is an example:

S C A R E and B O A T become (_CARE_) and (_BOAST_)

70.   B E A R and R I N G   become (________) and (________)

71.   S T E A K and O U G H T become (________) and (________)

72.   B E A R D and C A T   become (________) and (________)

73.   C A N O E and B U T   become (________) and (________)

74.   S C A L E and L A Y   become (________) and (________)

75.   S P I E D and M O S T   become (________) and (________)

There are 5 children Alan, Beth, Chris, David and Edward, who are all different ages. Chris is the oldest and is one year older than Edward who is two years older than Beth. Beth is 9 and is one year older than David who is 2 years younger than Alan.
Now answer the following questions:

76.   How old is Chris? . . . . (________)

77.   Who is the youngest? . . . .   (________)

78.   How much older than David is Chris? . . . .   (________)

79.   When Edward is 17 how old will Beth be? . . . .   (________)

80.   How many years are there between Edward and Alan? . . .   (________)

The number codes for three of the following four words are given below. These codes are not written in the same order as the words and one of the codes is missing.

ROSE   TOES   SORE   TOSS
7485   8475   3457

Work out the correct code for each word and answer the following questions by writing your answers in the brackets.

81.   What is the code for the word TESTER? . . . .   (____________)

82.   What is the code for the word RESTS? . . . .   (____________)

83.   What is the code for the word SETTER? . . . .   (____________)

84.   What word has the number code 358848? . . . .   (____________)

85.   What word has the number code 748358? . . . .   (____________)

86.   What word has the number code 8447358? . . . . . .   (____________)

Fill in the missing word in brackets which is needed to complete the third pair of words. This is formed in the same way as the second word in each of the first two pairs of words. Here is an example:

pear   reap   /   dear   read   /   lead   (_deal_)

87.   hate   heat   /   pale   peal   /   feel   (________)

88.   motor   rot   /   kites   set   /   wider   (________)

89.   tales   stale   /   angled   dangle   /   anger   (________)

90.   spoon   son   /   beast   bat   /   meant   (________)

91.   borrow   bow   /   biting   big   /   pantry   (________)

92.   create   cat   /   feline   fin   /   polite   (________)

Underline ONE word inside the brackets which CANNOT be made using the letters of the word in capitals outside the brackets.

93.   CHARACTER   (reach   crater   teacher   earth   cheat)

94.   ATMOSPHERE   (poster   paste   phrase   master   spread)

95.   CONCENTRATE   (centre   ocean   tract   street   concrete)

96.   DESCRIPTION   (notice   prince   tepid   direction   portion)

97.   PURCHASES   (shares   spruce   sharp   patch   purse)

The following are a type of simple crossword. Complete each puzzle by fitting the five words on the right-hand side of the grid horizontally and vertically into the correct positions. One word has already been included. Here is an example:

S	O	N

ASP
END
TOO
POD
ATE

becomes

A	*T*	*E*
S	*O*	*N*
P	*O*	*D*

98.

A	R	E

PAY
YEN
IRE
PEN
PIP

99.

		K
		E
		G

SEA
SEE
HAG
ASK
ASH

100.

P	E	N

ICE
ACE
DEN
LAP
LID

YOU HAVE COMPLETED THE TEST

GO BACK AND CHECK

REMEMBER : CHECKING MEANS RETHINKING

GRADED TEST PAPER 10

NAME . . . .

DATE . . . .

Instructions:

1.   Allow 50 minutes for this Test.

2.   Work quickly and accurately in PENCIL.

3.   Always write NEATLY. If you need to change an answer cross out clearly so your examiner can see easily what you intend your answer to be. Do not use an eraser.

4.   Always read the instructions of EACH question carefully so you know precisely what you are expected to do. Underline or write your answer in the brackets provided.

5.   Use the edges of the pages for the Technique/working out.

6.   Try to answer ALL the questions. Remember you can only get marks for the questions you answer!

7.   Do not spend longer than 30 seconds on any question you cannot do. Move on. Keep up your speed. Don't get behind.

8.   Circle the number of any question you miss out. When you finish your paper, return quickly to these. Do these first. Finally, return to the beginning of the paper. Check rigorously all your answers.

   Remember: CHECKING MEANS RETHINKING.

9.   Your Examiner should tell you when you are half way through, 10 minutes, 5 minutes, 2 minutes and 1 minute to go.

10. Use all the 50 minutes. DO NOT stop working or checking until you are told to stop.

SCORE:

In each of the following number series there is a different connection between the numbers. Find each connection and continue the series placing your answer in the brackets.

1. 4 6 9 (_____) 18 24

2. 3 9 27 (_____) 243

3. 7 8 (_____) 16 23 (_____)

4. 9 11 14 18 (_____) 29

5. 168 84 (_____) 21 (_____)

6. 11 8 12 9 13 (_____) 14 (_____)

7. 480 96 24 8 (_____)

Sara, James, Christopher, Simone and Khaled decided to raise some money for charity. Sara, Simone and James organised a raffle. Christopher, Khaled and Sara collected jumble for a car boot sale. Christopher, Simone and James organised a sponsored walk and everyone except Khaled sold cakes at a cake stall. Now answer the following questions:

8. Who collected jumble for a car boot sale and did not help at the cake stall? . . . . (____________)

9. Who organised a sponsored walk, sold cakes and collected jumble for a car boot sale? . . . . (____________)

10. How many children helped with a cake sale but could not take part in a sponsored walk? . . . . (____________)

11. Who did neither a sponsored walk nor a cake sale?. (____________)

12. How many children helped with a raffle, helped with a cake sale and took part on a sponsored walk? . . . . (____________)

Five children did a test for which 100 marks were awarded. Louise gained 96 marks. Jacob had half as many as the person who came top. John lost 6 marks. David had 8 marks fewer than John and Sara had 10 marks fewer than Louise. Now answer the following questions:

13. Who came top? . . . . (____________)

14. Which two children had the same mark? . . . . . (____________)

---

15. Who came second ? . . . .   (________________)

16. What was the difference between Jacob's and
    John's marks? . . . .   (________________)

**In the following sentences the word written on the left-hand side of
the page has had its letters jumbled up. Unjumble the letters and
write the correct word in the brackets:**

17.   R S C U C I   Clowns are found here. . .   (________________)

18. M C Y S O A R E   A type of tree . . . .   (________________)

19.   R P U S T O   A kind of vegetable . . . . .   (________________)

20. L D R C A E A N   An annual timetable . . . .   (________________)

21.   L O S T O   You can sit on this . . . . . .   (________________)

22.   D Y R I A   A daily record . . . .   (________________)

**Put the following words into alphabetical order by writing the
numbers 1, 2, 3, 4 and 5 in the brackets which follow the words:**

23. string ( )   stripe ( )   strength ( )   strike ( )   strong ( )

24. funnel ( )   furrow ( )   fury ( )   furlong ( )   fuss ( )

25. harbour ( )   harrow ( )   harp ( )   hangar ( )   harness ( )

26. dossier ( )   donkey ( )   document ( )   donor ( )   doctor ( )

27. flash ( )   flag ( )   fragrant ( )   flick ( )   fling ( )

**In the following questions imagine the words are written
BACKWARDS and then arranged in alphabetical order.
Now underline the correct answers in the brackets:**

28. Which of these words would come THIRD?
                            (meant   sent   consent   dissent   comment)

29. Which of these words would come FOURTH?
                    (dictation   separation   commendation   ration   saturation)

30. Which of these words would come SECOND?
                            (starving   sting   fling   flying   starling)

---

31.   Which of these words would come THIRD?

(babies   ladies   dies   rubies   tries)

32.   Which of these words would come FOURTH?

(constable   reasonable   sensible   terrible   edible)

A B C D E F G H I J K L M N O P Q R S T U V W X Y Z

The above alphabet is to help you with the following code questions. Write the answers in the brackets. Here is an example:

If G B S N means F A R M what does N J M L mean. . . (_MILK_)

33.   If B O O K is written C Q R O then R E A D is   . . .   (___________)

34.   If D O G is written 4 15 7 then C A T is . . . .   (___________)

35.   If G O A T is written T L Z G then L A M B is . . . . .   (___________)

36.   If B V S F means C U T E then R X D F S means . .   (___________)

37.   If G 15 T 19 D is H O U S E then F 1 Q 4 D 14 is . . .   (___________)

38.   If C X A Y T Z means C A T then P X I Y G Z means   (___________)

In the following sentences there is a FOUR-letter word hidden between words which are next to each other. Find the word and write it in the brackets. Here is an example:

Scientific paper*s and* books . . . .(_sand_)

39.   The oranges are already ripe. . . . .   (___________)

40.   The sea is so low . . . .   (___________)

41.   This chair is too low to sit on . . . .   (___________)

42.   Boys and girls come out to play . . . .   (___________)

43.   The flower bed is heavy with dew . . . .   (___________)

44.   The football missed the net . . . .   (___________)

The following questions are concerned with numbers. Work out the correct answer and write this number in the brackets.

45.   14 is two more than half this number . . . . (________)

46.   24 is 4 more than twice this number . . . . (________)

47.   If I add 2 and subtract 7 from this number the answer is 15   (________)

48.   150 is 10 times larger than this number . . . . (________)

49.   If I add this number to the number of days in a
      week the answer is 23 . . . . (________)

50.   If I multiply this number by 4 and subtract 7 the
      answer is 25 . . . . (________)

51.   26 is 8 less than twice this number . . . . (________)

A B C D E F G H I J K L M N O P Q R S T U V W X Y Z

The following rows of letters have a different rule governing each line. Work out each rule and write in the brackets the next letter or letters in the series. The above alphabet will help you.

52.   A P   C N   E L   G J   (______)   K F

53.   B O   E M   H K   K I   N G   (______)

54.   A B   E D   I F   M H   (______)   U L

55.   F Y   (______)   J U   L S   N Q   (______)

56.   L A   M C   K F   N J   (______)   (______)

57.   A C E   (______)   E G I   G I K   (______)

---

58.   **If flour is more expensive than sugar but cheaper than butter, underline the ONE sentence below which must be true:**

      a.   Flour is the most expensive.
      b.   Sugar is sweet.
      c.   Butter is cheaper than flour.
      d.   Sugar is the cheapest.

In each of the following questions you must change one letter in the top word to make a new sensible word. By changing a different letter in this new word it is possible to make the bottom word which is given. Write out the sensible word on the line provided.
Here is an example:

<table>
<tr><td>R O A D</td><td></td><td>R O A D</td></tr>
<tr><td>————</td><td>becomes</td><td>*R O A M*</td></tr>
<tr><td>F O A M</td><td></td><td>F O A M</td></tr>
</table>

Now answer the following questions:

59. M A K E	60. C O M B	61. B E A T	62. H A N D
————	————	————	————
C A P E	D O M E	R E S T	H A R E

In the following questions the three words on the right go together in the same way as the three words on the left. However, the middle word of the three on the right is missing. Write the missing word in the brackets.

63.   HOSE   (S O A P)   CAPE   :   LEST   (________)   MATE

64.   MAIN   (M I S T)   SEAT   :   CHOP   (________)   SOOT

65.   RACE   (S C A R)   SACK   :   MARE   (________)   PERT

66.   CART   (T E A R)   EVER   :   OWES   (________)   EVES

67.   VASE   (E V E R)   TEAR   :   REST   (________)   LAMP

68.   CARD   (D R A G)   RAGE   :   MAIL   (________)   ANDS

In each of the following questions write the SAME letter in both brackets. This letter should end BOTH of the first words and begin BOTH of the second words of each pair.

69.   C A R   (___)   R U M   :   S E N   (___)   A R T

70.   L I S   (___)   A L E   :   H A R   (___)   L U S

71.   C O M   (___)   R I M   :   L I M   (___)   L U E

72.	T O O (___) R U E	:	F E L (___) I M E
73.	L I S (___) O O L	:	C A M (___) A C K
74.	M E S (___) A N D	:	W I T (___) I N D
75.	T R A C (___) I N D	:	T R U C (___) N E W

The number codes for three of the following four words are given below. These codes are not written in the same order as the words and one of the codes is missing.

TEAM   MEAN   MANE   NAME
6487   6748   9746

Work out the correct code for each word and answer the following questions by writing your answer in the brackets.

76.   What is the code for the word TENANT? . . . . (______________)

77.   What is the code for the word MEANT? . . . . (______________)

78.   What is the code for the word TAME? . . . . (______________)

79.   What word has the number code 8749? . . . . (______________)

80.   What word has the number code 6497? . . . . (______________)

Using the letter codes above, work out the following sums. Give each answer as a LETTER.

81. A x M – E – T . . . . (________)

82. N x M ÷ A – N . . . . (________)

83. A x T ÷ M . . . . (________)

There are two groups of words in each question below. Choose TWO words, one from each group which are OPPOSITE in meaning. Here is an example:

look / observe / _obstruct_ : _assist_ / impede / watch

84.   loose / lenient / slack   :   limp / easy / severe

85.   study / party / frivolous   :   hard / serious / fun

86.   demean / demand / please :   delight / humble / dignify

---

87.　profound / great / abundance　　:　scarcity / plentiful / numerous

88.　　open / opulent / opposite　　:　rich / poor / near

In each of the following sentences there are two words which should change places with each other to make a sensible sentence. Underline the two words. Here is an example:

Put the _table_ under the _shoes_.

89.　Forty three and thirty two make seventy one.

90.　If tomorrow is Tuesday yesterday was Thursday.

91.　Is the storm the sea during rough.

92.　Is a there man in the moon?

93.　Tomorrow is yesterday's today.

94.　With teacher is pleased the the class.

95.　The steam came into the kettle and out the air.

One of the words in each of the following sentences has THREE consecutive letters missing. Without changing the order of these three letters they spell another proper word. Write this word in the brackets. Here is an example:

~~millions~~
There are mions of people in London. .(_ _ill_ _)

96.　IIe placed a std of his hair under the microscope . . . .　(_________)

97.　He found it difficult to fas his buttons quickly . . . .　(_________)

98.　The horse is in the sle for the night . . . .　(_________)

99.　He lised carefully to what the teacher said . . . .　(_________)

100. Josie went in the kitchen caet for a cup . . . .　(_________)

YOU HAVE COMPLETED THE TEST

GO BACK AND CHECK

REMEMBER : CHECKING MEANS RETHINKING

PRIZE CERTIFICATE

Pupil's Name: ....

This is to certify that the above-named pupil has completed Verbal Reasoning Graded Test Papers 2
and has achieved

a BEST SCORE of .... within the time allowed.

I .... (Parent)

am extremely proud of these achievements and undertake to

(insert details of Special Award) ....

....

....

in recognition of this achievement and to show my appreciation of all the hard work and effort that has gone into
doing so well.

Well Done!
Congratulations!

ADDITIONAL EXERCISES

Additional exercises to improve your child's speed and accuracy.

**A.	To improve ability to listen to instructions and carry them out quickly and accurately.**

Take any story book, and ask your child to find certain things in it, for instance:

a.	What is the third word on the fourth line on page 15?

b.	How many letters are in the last word on the bottom of page 16?

c.	How many vowels are there in the seventh word on the fourteenth line of page 10?

d.	How many a's are there in the sixth word on the ninth line on page 7, and so on.

**B.	To improve your child's ability to work through the alphabet quickly and accurately.**

Take a dictionary and ask your child to open the page at the letter 'M', 'N', 'B' and so on, so he learns to judge the position of the letters in the alphabet and is able to estimate where to open the dictionary to find a particular letter.

**C.	To give your child a concept of 30 seconds and so be able to pace himself in an examination that requires him to answer one question in 30 seconds.**

a.	While checking with your own watch ask your child to tell you when he thinks 30 seconds has passed. Repeat until he can judge it accurately within 5 seconds either side.

b.	'Speed handwriting' - see how many times he can write his name in 30 seconds. Try again. Can he improve his 'record'? Many children I have taught can achieve up to 30 five-letter words in 30 seconds!

TRY TO AWAKEN YOUR CHILD'S INNATE SPEED
WHILE MAINTAINING ACCURACY.

PERSONAL RECORD TABLE

GRADED TEST PAPERS 2

Name: ....

DATE	PAPER NO.	SCORE	COMMENTS
	6		
	7		
	8		
	9		
	10		

How to fill in your child's PERSONAL RECORD TABLE:

Fill in the DATE of the Test Paper in Column One.

Enter your child's SCORE in Column Three.

Identify those questions your child has answered incorrectly (or is having difficulty with).

Record in the COMMENTS section above the TYPE and BOOK REFERENCE indicated against those Answers.

Revise the TECHNIQUE and do the PRACTICE EXERCISES and the FURTHER PRACTICE EXERCISES of those Types.

At some convenient time after the revision ask your child to resit the Test Paper to confirm his understanding and application of the Technique. (Note and reward the improved score on the resit!)

ANSWERS

TEST PAPER 10:

1. 13
2. 81
3. 11 32
4. 23
5. 42 10.5
6. 10 11
7. 4 T26/3
8. Khaled
9. Christopher
10. 1
11. [illegible]
12. 2 [illegible]
13. Louise
14. Sara and David
15. John
16. 46 T30/3
17. CIRCUS
18. SYCAMORE
19. SPROUT

20. CALENDAR
21. STOOL
22. DIARY T19/2
23. 3 4 1 2 5
24. 1 3 4 2 5
25. 2 5 4 1 3
26. 5 3 2 4 1
27. 2 1 5 3 4 T17/2
28. sent
29. saturation
30. starling
31. dies
32. terrible T17/2
33. S G D H
34. [illegible]
35. [illegible]
36. SWEET
37. GARDEN
38. PIG T32/4
39. real
40. solo

41. tool
42. sand
43. dish
44. then T5/1
45. 24
46. 10
47. 20
48. 15
49. 16
50. 8
51. 17 T24/3
52. IH
53. QE
54. QJ
55. HW PO
56. JO OU
57. CEG IKM T16/2
58. [illegible] T31/4
59. CAKE
60. COME
61. BEST

62. HARD T6/1
63. SEAT
64. COST
65. PRAM
66. SEWS
67. TRAP
68. LAND T22/2
69. D
70. P
71. B
72. T
73. P
74. H
75. K T21/2
76. 978489
77. 67489
78. 9467
79. NEAT
80. MATE
81. [illegible]
82. A

83. M T33/4
84. lenient severe
85. frivolous serious
86. demean dignify
87. abundance scarcity
88. opulent poor T7/1
89. three one
90. Tuesday Thursday
91. is during
92. there a
93. tomorrow today
94. with the (1st)
95. into out T1/1
96. ran
97. ten
98. tab
99. ten
100. bin T20/2

TYPE / BOOK REFERENCE

Alongside each section of Answers is a Reference Number e.g. T26/3.
The T reference refers to TYPE number.
The last digit identifies in which of the four books of TECHNIQUE
and PRACTICE the Type can be found.